# A NOTE TO PARENTS

When your children are ready to "step into reading," giving them the right books—and lots of them—is as crucial as giving them the right food to eat. **Step into Reading Books** present exciting stories and information reinforced with lively, colorful illustrations that make learning to read fun, satisfying, and worthwhile. They are priced so that acquiring an entire library of them is affordable. And they are beginning readers with an important difference—they're written on four levels.

**Step 1 Books,** with their very large type and extremely simple vocabulary, have been created for the very youngest readers. **Step 2 Books** are both longer and slightly more difficult. **Step 3 Books,** written to mid-second-grade reading levels, are for the child who has acquired even greater reading skills. **Step 4 Books** offer exciting nonfiction for the increasingly proficient reader.

Children develop at different ages. **Step into Reading Books,** with their four levels of reading, are designed to help children become good—and interested—readers *faster*. The grade levels assigned to the four steps—preschool through grade 1 for Step 1, grades 1 through 3 for Step 2, grades 2 and 3 for Step 3, and grades 2 through 4 for Step 4—are intended only as guides. Some children move through all four steps very rapidly; others climb the steps over a period of several years. These books will help your child "step into reading" in style!

*For Artemis and Austin, and for all
the kids at Fort River Elementary School,
short, tall, and in-between*

# A Step 2 Book

Text copyright © 1995 by Corinne Demas Bliss
Illustrations copyright © 1995 by Nancy Poydar
All rights reserved under International and Pan-American Copyright Conventions.
Published in the United States by Random House, Inc., New York, and simultaneously
in Canada by Random House of Canada Limited, Toronto.
http://www.randomhouse.com/

*Library of Congress Cataloging-in-Publication Data*
Bliss, Corinne Demas. The shortest kid in the world / by Corinne Demas Bliss.
p. cm. — (Step into reading. A Step 2 book)  SUMMARY: Emily is unhappy with her size until
a new girl in class helps her see that being short can have its advantages.
ISBN: 0-679-85809-1 (trade) — ISBN: 0-679-95809-6 (lib. bdg.)
[1. Size—Fiction. 2. Schools—Fiction. 3. Self-acceptance—Fiction.]  I. Title.  II. Series: Step
into reading. Step 2 book.  PZ7.B61917Sh  1995  [E]—dc20  93-45421

Printed in the United States of America 10 9 8 7 6 5
STEP INTO READING is a trademark of Random House, Inc.

Step into Reading™

# THE SHORTEST KID IN THE WORLD

by Corinne Demas Bliss

illustrated by Nancy Poydar

Random House 🏠 New York

Emily was the shortest kid
in her class.

Emily was the shortest kid

on her school bus.

Emily was the shortest kid
in her family.

"I'm the shortest kid
in the whole world!" cried Emily.
It wasn't true,
but she felt that way.

The kids in her class
called her Shrimp.

The kids on the school bus
called her Peewee.

Her parents called her Peanut.

Her big brother called her Munchkin.

Her little brother

called her Munchkin, too.

He was taller

than she was.

Emily hated being short.

Especially at school.

She couldn't drink
from the water fountain
without wetting her shirt.

In the library,

she couldn't reach the books

on the top shelf.

She couldn't see

over anyone's head

at the puppet show.

Brian teased her in the coatroom.

"Shrimp!" he said,

and he wriggled his nose.

Emily hated being called Shrimp.

"Don't worry about it,"

said Emily's mother.

"You'll grow."

Which was true, of course.

But everyone else

was growing, too.

Emily was afraid

she'd never catch up.

Emily decided to do something
about it herself.

She drank lots of milk.

She ate lots of spinach.

She did stretching exercises
in her room every night.

She wore her hair puffed up
on the top.

She got new shoes
with thick soles.
She walked
with her head held up
as high as she could.

But she was still
the shortest kid
in her class.

At least that was true
until Marietta Fairchild
moved to town.
Marietta Fairchild had long hair
and a deep voice.
She had a dozen pencils
with her name printed on them
in gold.
When they lined up for recess,
Marietta stepped in front.
"Since I'm the shortest
person in the class,"
she announced,
"I get to lead the line."

"Are you shorter than I am?"

Emily asked, hopefully.

"Of course I am!"

said Marietta Fairchild.

"I'm a whole inch shorter

than you are—at least."

Marietta asked Brian to get a ruler.

He measured them back to back.

It turned out Marietta was right.

"But we don't line up

for recess by size," said Emily.

"Perhaps you don't,"
said Marietta Fairchild.
"But it's always polite
to let the shortest person
go first."

When they got drinks

from the water fountain,

Marietta didn't wet her shirt.

She used a cup.

"Because I'm short

I get to keep my own cup

at school," she said.

Ms. Dever, their teacher,
let her move her desk
to the front of the classroom.

"So I can see

the blackboard better,"

said Marietta.

In the library,

Marietta got to use the rolling ladder

so she could pick out books

from the top shelf.

No one called her Peewee

or Munchkin or Shrimp.

Not even Brian.

Everyone called her Marietta.

"Shortest is bestest,"

said Marietta.

That night Emily's mother
asked about the new girl in class.

"She's shorter than I am,"
said Emily.
"Well, that's nice,"
said her mother.
"You're not
the shortest one anymore."
Emily didn't say anything.

At dinner

she didn't touch her spinach.

She didn't drink her milk.

She didn't do any stretching exercises.

The next morning,

Emily brushed her hair

straight down.

She wet the top

so it lay flat

on her head.

She wore her slip-on shoes
with the thin soles.

But Marietta was still shorter.

Emily slumped her shoulders.

She pulled in her neck

like a turtle.

"Are you feeling all right, Emily?"
asked Ms. Dever.

"Yes," said Emily.

In the coatroom after school,

Marietta sat next to Emily

while they put on their boots.

"I'm sorry you're not

the shortest one

in the class anymore,"

said Marietta.

"But can we still be friends?"

"Okay," said Emily.

"Good!" said Marietta.

"Why don't you ask Ms. Dever
   if you can move your desk
   next to mine?"

Emily smiled.

"All right," she said.

"See you tomorrow, Shrimp!"

said Brian.

"My name is Emily," said Emily.

"Hi, Munchkin," said Emily's little

brother when she got home.

"My name is Emily," said Emily.

"How was your day, Peanut?"

asked her mother.

"My name is Emily," said Emily,

in a Marietta sort of voice.

"And I'd prefer

to be called that way."

At school the next day,
Emily moved her desk
next to Marietta's.

Soon they became best friends.

Then Marietta started to grow.

By March she was only

a little bit shorter

than Emily.

By April she was only

a tiny bit shorter

than Emily.

By May she was almost

the same size.

By June she *was*

the same size.

Maybe even taller.

Brian got the ruler.

He measured them

back to back.

Emily was shorter!

"Shrimp!" cried Brian.

"Shortest is bestest!" said Emily.

But then she looked again at Brian.

Something funny had happened.

She and Marietta had both grown a lot.

But Brian hadn't grown much at all.

Emily got the ruler.

Marietta measured Brian and Emily
back to back.

"Brian's shorter!" cried Marietta.

"Shrimp!" cried Emily.

"Shortest is bestest," said Brian.

And they all laughed.

Now Brian was the shortest kid

in the class.

At least he was until September.

Then somebody else got a turn.